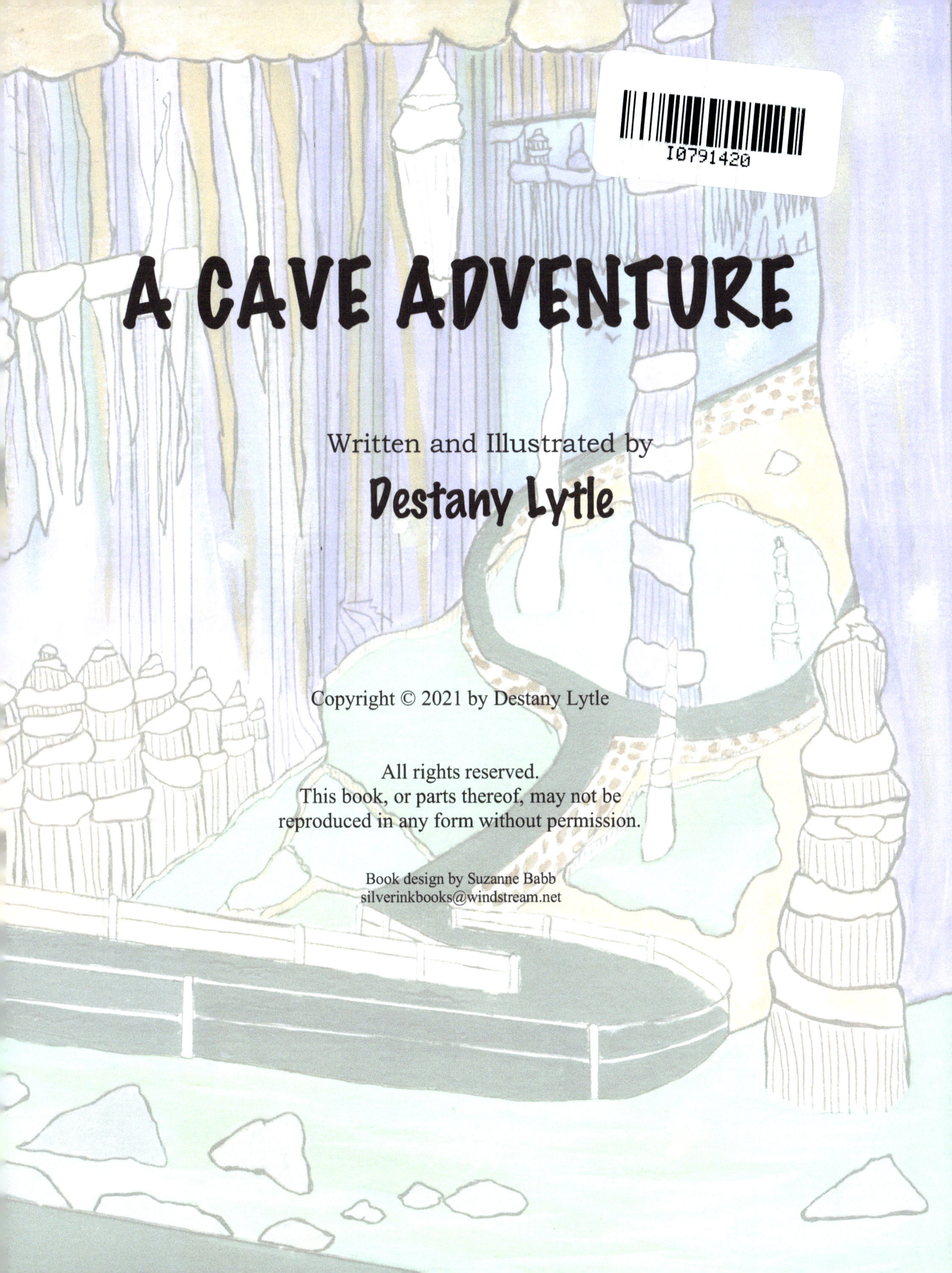

A CAVE ADVENTURE

Written and Illustrated by

Destany Lytle

Copyright © 2021 by Destany Lytle

Book design by Suzanne Babb
silverinkbooks@windstream.net

For every child. You are incredibly loved! May you never lose your sense of wonder and may you always seek adventures.

- *Destany*

Blake's teacher, Mrs. Becky, stood in front of the class and made an announcement.

"We are going on a field trip to Blanchard Springs Caverns! Be sure to wear a jacket and tennis shoes because the cave temperature is 58 degrees and the walkways will be damp."

All the students buzzed with excitement except for Blake. When he heard the word cave, he had a million questions that he believed only one person could answer. But then a sudden thought scared him stiff and kept him from raising his hand. Blake had a secret. He was afraid of bats.

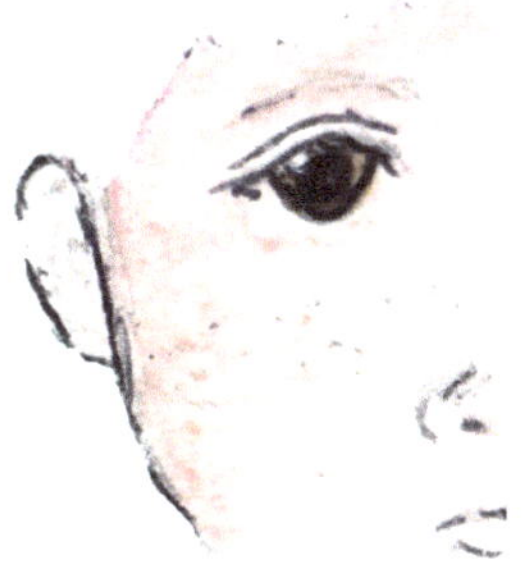

The next day, while Blake was riding the bus to the cave, the thought of bats made him feel uneasy. He wondered if a bat would try to fly in his hair, or worse would it try to suck his blood?

His thoughts were interrupted by Mrs. Becky's voice. "We're here," she called out.

She led the students across a concrete bridge and into a tall wooden building where a man was waiting for them at the front desk.

"Hello!" the man's voice boomed. "We've been waiting for you all morning. Aren't you here to help mop the floors?"

The students eyed their teacher. She gave them a smile and their looks dissolved into laughter. "No!" they chimed together.

"You're not? Oh, that's right, you're here to help clean the bathrooms."

The students laughed even louder and gave out a long "Noooooo!"

"Hmm, so what are you here for?"

The students beamed, "To see the cave!"

"Well in that case, ladies and gentleman, I will be your tour guide today. My name is Paul."

Paul led them down the central hallway, through a set of glass doors, and into a small elevator lobby. Blake followed close behind him.

In the lobby, Paul discussed the rules. He explained that no one should touch the formations because it would prevent them from growing.

"Why would they stop growing?" Blake inquired.

"Good question! Our skin has acids, oils, and salts and when we touch a formation those are left behind in our fingerprints. The formation grows as water drips or flows over it depositing a mineral called Calcite. Water and oil don't mix, so when we touch a formation we waterproof it. Thus, we keep it from ever growing again. Usually we don't have to worry about the kids though. It's the adults we have to keep an eye on. So, I'll need you to be my policeman and ensure that no adult touches the cave today on our tour."

The students smiled and gave their teacher the *I'm watching you* sign with their fingers. She laughed and promised not to touch the cave.

Paul asked, "Are there any more questions?"

Blake wanted to ask about the bats, but he decided not to.

The students loaded into the elevator and started their descent. "Alright, since there are no more questions we are going to drop down 216 feet. That is equivalent to a 21 and ½ story building! All aboard," Paul called out.

In the elevator, Paul made Blake laugh so much that he almost forgot about the possibility of seeing bats.

Blake looked up at him. Paul's rosy cheeks and bright blue eyes shined through his gold framed glasses. He had salt and pepper colored hair with a snowy white beard. It reminded Blake of Santa Claus except Paul wore a green suit instead of a red one.

At the bottom, they stepped into a dark lobby. Paul directed them to a glass door. He opened it with a loud screech. Everyone squeezed inside and Mrs. Becky closed the door behind them. At the end of the narrow hall was a second door.

Paul leaned against it. "Boys and girls, welcome to Blanchard Springs Caverns! He opened the glass door and the students gasped in bewilderment. Cave curtains hugged the walls in glistening waves. Twinkling towers hung from the ceiling and rose up from the floor. It was a sparkling, underground wonderland.

"This is the Cathedral Room," said Paul as he waved his hand across the room. It is 1,150 feet long, close to the length of four football fields. At the center is the Giant Column that is 65 feet tall!"

Off to his left, Blake noticed something fluttering around in swift motions. He froze, halting the line of students behind him. Paul put his hand on Blake's shoulder and gave him a wink.

"This is the perfect place for me to tell a cheesy cave joke. Does anyone want to hear it?"

"Yes!" the students shouted.

"What is the first thing a bat learns in school?" Paul asked. He paused, then said loudly, "The alphaBAT!"

The cave reverberated with the sounds of the student's laughter that echoed around the delicate formations.

"I know you may have heard some bad things about bats, but in our next room I hope to dispel some of those myths."

Blake was hesitant to move, but the man's smile reassured him so he followed Paul to the next room.

Paul pointed. "This is the Coral Room."

They were hemmed in by flowstone in every direction. It looked as if this is where a giant would get his ice cream. Chocolate and vanilla scoops toppled over each other melting into a sea of sparkles.

The cave livened the student's imagination. One pointed, "I see jellyfish on the wall!"

Another called out, "I see a horse on the ceiling!"

Paul lowered his voice to a whisper and the students listened intently...

"So, *what are your questions about bats?*"

Blake slowly raised his hand. "Do they try to suck your blood or fly in your hair?"

"Great question, and the answer is no. There is a type of bat that drinks blood, it is named the Vampire bat. It doesn't really suck blood. It makes a small cut and licks the blood from its prey. However, those are found in South America and usually don't bother humans. It drinks blood from cows, pigs, and birds, but they don't even feel it. There are five species of bats that live here at Blanchard. They are the Big Brown, Little Brown, Indiana, Tricolor, and Grey bats."

"How many of you love mosquitos?"

When no one raised their hand, Paul said, "That means you must love bats! If you hold up your thumb, that is the average size of our bat and that single bat consumes 1,000 to 3,000 insects every night! Mosquitos are one of the bugs on their menu!"

Paul continued, "I love bats! My favorite thing about them is their POOP."

"Gross", the students protested.

"It's true! A white fungus will grow on fresh guano or bat poop. A world of microorganisms thrives there! This is the beginning of the cave's food chain. The isopods feed on the microorganisms, the crickets feed on the isopods, and it goes all the way to the T-Rex of the cave…. our six inch Cave Salamander! So here is my question for you, what would happen if we lost our bats?"

Blake's hand shot up!

"Yes, sir," Paul called.

"If the bats were gone, there would be no more poop, and after that everything else would die."

"That's right! The bats are responsible for all the biodiversity in our cave!"

Blake thought about it, and he decided that bats were pretty important.

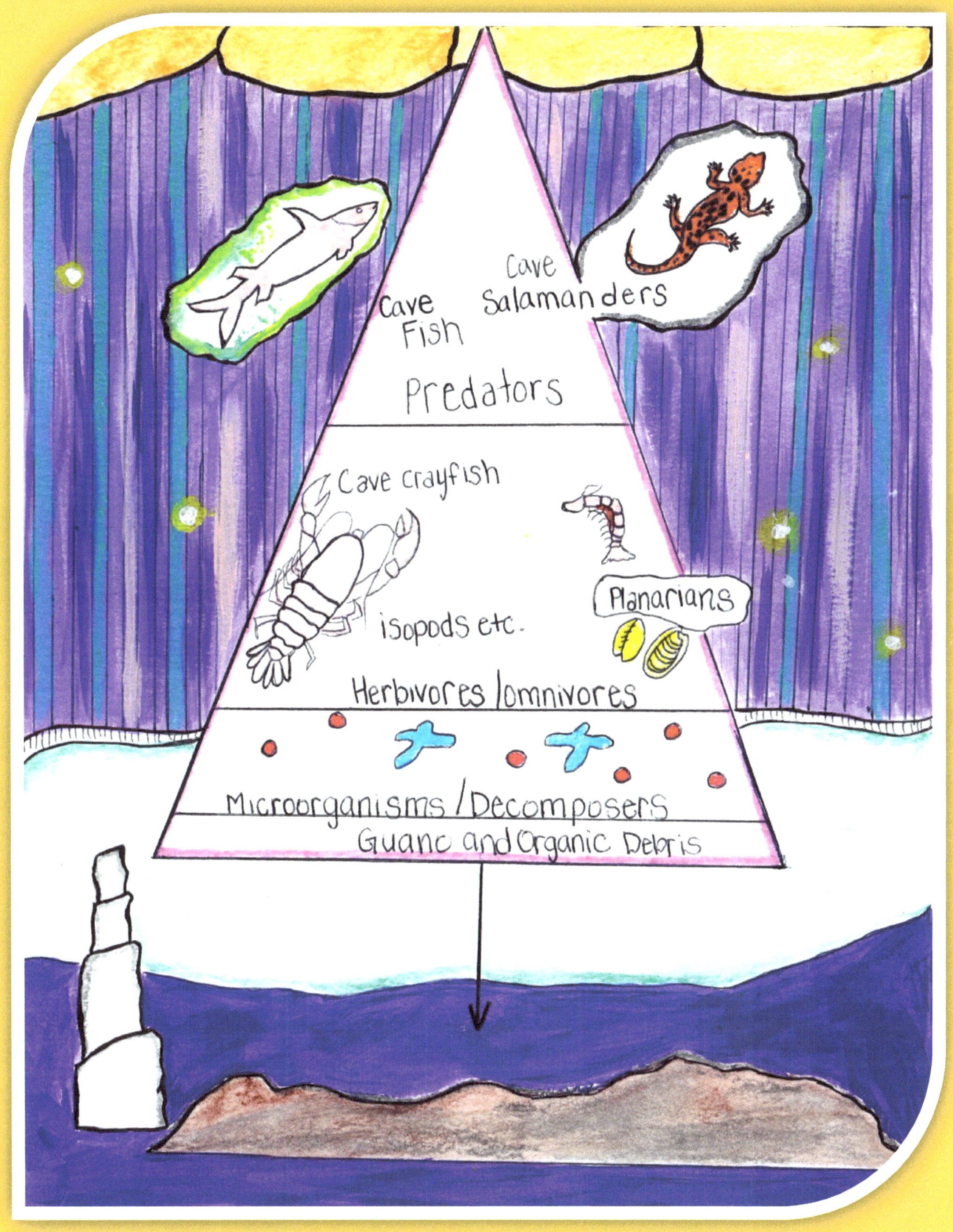

Cave Fish
Cave Salamanders
Predators
Cave crayfish
Planarians
isopods etc.
Herbivores /omnivores
Microorganisms /Decomposers
Guano and Organic Debris

"Alright, we have one last room to see!"

Paul led the way, until he stopped on a platform next to a light switch. He waited for all the students to circle round.

"Geologists believe that this cave is around 50 million years old! The formations that we've seen today are anywhere from 2-million to 5-million years old. That makes it very special. It was here before my name was called into existence and it will be here long after I'm gone. That means we need you to protect it and all the creatures inside for the next generation. On that note, I present to you… the Soda Straw room."

Paul flipped the switch and light flooded the room.

The students drank in the beauty of it. Hundreds of pure white stalactites pointed down from the ceiling to their sister stalagmites who reached up from the floor. It was an utter forest of formations blanketed in snowy crystals. Blake looked at the room and knew right away he had never seen anything more magnificent.

As the students were preparing to leave, Blake asked Mrs. Becky if he could tell Paul something really fast! She agreed, and he walked over to Paul, then tugged on his sleeve.

Paul turned. "Yes, sir, do you have a question?"

Blake shook his head. "No. I just wanted to tell you something. I'm not afraid of bats anymore and I promise to protect the cave!"

"I'm so proud to hear that." Paul smiled and his blue eyes shined.

Blake gave Paul a big hug and then rejoined his school group.

On the way home, Blake looked out the window and saw something small and brown fluttering swiftly through the sky. He smiled as the bat disappeared in the distance.

Author's Note

Paul McIntosh was born April 6th, 1957. He had a reverence for nature from the very beginning! In 2002, Paul began working for the US Forest Service as a Tour Guide at Blanchard Springs Caverns.

Paul was loved by his fellow employees as well as the public. He was an amazing human being who loved kids, adventure, and caves. He had a kindred spirit with an ability to brighten anyone's day. I will always remember his bright eyes that made others feel cheerful, his infinite supply of cheesy jokes that never lost their luster, his shared stories of past caving adventures, and above all his love for his caving family and the cave itself.

Paul is remembered fondly by all those who were privileged to know him. He spent his life doing what he was most passionate about, caving. In addition, he was a lifelong learner. Paul left a legacy of light and love. His life is a lesson to us all that we should pursue our passions, be a good steward to nature, and ALWAYS be full of wonder.

I hope that this book allowed you to experience the character of a man who was like magic in his ability to bring joy to all those around him.

Celebrating the life of Paul.

May your new adventure be the best one yet.

About the Author

Destany Lytle has a seasonal office that is 216 feet underground! In the summers you can almost always find her leading tours at Blanchard Springs Caverns.

When she is not caving, she can be found in a classroom. Destany is a proud educator. She teaches reading at Midland Elementary. Kids and caves are her world!

In addition, Destany is a member of the National Speleological Society (a group that studies caves).

She resides in Arkansas.

www.ingramcontent.com/pod-product-compliance
Lightning Source LLC
Chambersburg PA
CBHW040207240726
48664CB00002B/860